This book belongs

_____

This book is dedicated to my children - Mikey, Kobe, and Jojo.

Taylor Swift

By Mary Nhin

Hi, I'm Taylor Swift.

I have a tale to tell you – a tale of melodies and challenges I faced along the way to making my dreams come true!

Once upon a time, in the cozy town of Reading, Pennsylvania, a little girl with big dreams was born. That little girl was me!

From the moment I could talk, I sang. I even sang to my pet cat, Mr. Whiskers. He was always my most enthusiastic audience member.

As a young girl, making friends didn't come easily to me.

One time, I invited several girls from my middle school to go shopping but they all said no. So I decided to go with my mom, but then we saw the whole group of friends there.

After this happened, I felt lonely and sad. One of the things that helped me during this difficult time was to write in my journal.

When I turned 14, I packed up my dreams and guitar and headed to Nashville, Tennessee – the land of country music. Breaking into the music industry wasn't easy. I faced rejection after rejection, but I refused to give up.

When I strummed my guitar, it felt like my fingers were dancing across the strings, creating melodies that twirled like leaves in a gentle autumn wind.

Even though record labels turned me down and some even tried to change who I was, I didn't let their words bring me down.

When I wrote, I poured my heart onto each page. My lyrics were like windows into my soul, revealing the hopes, dreams, and fears of a young girl.

If you are lucky enough to find something that you love, and you have a shot at being good at it, don't stop ...

In Nashville, I strummed my guitar and sang my heart out at every opportunity I got. From small cafes to local talent shows, I shared my music with anyone who would listen. And you know what? People started to take notice! Soon, I was signed by a record label.

With my first album, "Taylor Swift," I introduced the world to my heartfelt lyrics and melodies. People started to resonate with the stories I told through my song-writing. I was so thankful when I was awarded a few Grammy Awards! But even as my songs rose up the charts, new challenges emerged.

As my fame grew, so did the criticism. People spread rumors about me. This made me want to shut the whole world out.

As I continued to grow and evolve as an artist, I decided to take a leap of faith and explore new musical territories. With albums like "Red" and "1989," I embraced pop music with open arms. And let me tell you, there's nothing more rewarding than knowing that my songs have touched the hearts of so many around the world.

I used my voice not just to sing, but to speak out for those who couldn't, standing up for what is right.

Over time, I grew as a business woman. I prompted awareness of intellectual property for musicians, reshaped ticketing models, and regularly used Easter eggs and cryptic teasers as a common practice in contemporary pop music.

Despite the challenges and setbacks, I never lost sight of who I was. I used my music as a tool to speak out against injustice, to empower others to embrace their uniqueness, and to spread love and kindness wherever I went. With each song I wrote and each stage I graced, I found strength in my voice.

I stayed true to myself and never forgot where I came from, always remembering the love and support of my family and fans.

Today, as I look back on my journey, I see that every challenge I faced was a stepping stone to success.

No matter what happens in life, be good to people. Being good to people is a wonderful legacy to leave behind.

Timeline

1989 – Taylor Alison Swift is born

2001 – Taylor learns to play the guitar

2006 – Taylor releases self-titled debut album

2007 – Taylor is awarded Horizon Award for best new artist

2008 – Taylor releases second album: "Fearless"

2009 – Taylor is awarded Album of the year ACM Award ("Fearless"); Taylor is awarded Video Music Award for best female video

2010 – Taylor wins 4 Grammys, including album of the year; Taylor releases third studio album: "Speak Now"

2011 – Taylor is awarded CMA entertainer of the year Award

2012 – Taylor releases fourth album: "Red"

2014 – Taylor releases fifth album: "1989"; Taylor wins album of the year Grammy Award for "1989"

2017 – Taylor releases sixth album: "Reputation"

2019 – Taylor releases seventh album: "Lover"

2020 – Taylor releases eighth and ninth albums: "Folklore" & "Evermore"; Taylor wins album of the year Grammy for "Folklore"; Taylor begins re-recording her earlier albums

2022 – Taylor releases tenth studio album: "Midnights"

2023 – Taylor receives 9 wins at the MTV Video Music Awards; Taylor becomes a billionaire

2024 – Taylor wins album of the year Grammy award for "Midnights"

I love hearing from my readers.
Write to me at info@ninjalifehacks.tv or send mail to:

Mary Nhin
5 West 15th St.
Edmond, OK 73013

Visit NinjaLifeHacks.tv for lesson plans and more!

 @marynhin   @officialninjalifehacks
#minimoversandshakers

 Ninja Life Hacks

 Mary Nhin   Ninja Life Hacks

 @officialninjalifehacks

64523257R00020